First World War
and Army of Occupation
War Diary
France, Belgium and Germany

29 DIVISION
87 Infantry Brigade,
Brigade Trench Mortar Battery
1 July 1916 - 31 August 1916

WO95/2305/7

The Naval & Military Press Ltd
www.nmarchive.com
Published in association with The National Archives

Published by

The Naval & Military Press Ltd

Unit 10 Ridgewood Industrial Park,

Uckfield, East Sussex,

TN22 5QE England

Tel: +44 (0) 1825 749494

www.naval-military-press.com

www.nmarchive.com

This diary has been reprinted in facsimile from the original. Any imperfections are inevitably reproduced and the quality may fall short of modern type and cartographic standards.

© Crown Copyright
Images reproduced by permission of The National Archives, London, England, 2015.

Contents

Document type	Place/Title	Date From	Date To
Heading	WO95/2305-7 87 Brigade Trench Mortar Battrey July '16-Aug '16		
Heading	29th Division 87th Infy Bde 87th Lt Trench Mortar Bty Jly-Aug 1916		
Heading	29th Division 87th Infantry Brigade. 87th Light Trench Mortar Battery July 1916		
War Diary	Trenches Q	01/07/1916	08/07/1916
War Diary	Acheux	09/07/1916	16/07/1916
War Diary	Trenches	17/07/1916	23/07/1916
War Diary	Bus	24/07/1916	24/07/1916
War Diary	Implier	25/07/1916	31/07/1916
Heading	29th Division. 87th Infantry Brigade. 87th Light Trench Mortar Battery August 1916		
Heading	War Diary of 87th T.M. Battery from Aug 1st to Aug. 31st 1916. (Volume 2)		
War Diary	Wieltje Sec. Trenches	01/08/1916	31/08/1916

WO/95/2305/7

87 Brigade Trench Mortar Battery

July '16 – Aug '16

29TH DIVISION
87TH INFY BDE

87TH LT TRENCH MORTAR BTY
JLY - AUG 1916

29th Division/6
87th Infantry Brigade.

87th LIGHT TRENCH MORTAR BATTERY

JULY 1916

Army Form C.

WAR DIARY
or
INTELLIGENCE SUMMARY
(Erase heading not required.)

87- T.M.B.

Instructions regarding War Diaries and Intelligence Summaries are contained in F. S. Regs., Part II. and the Staff Manual respectively. Title pages will be prepared in manuscript.

Place	Date	Hour	Summary of Events and Information	Remarks and references to Appendices
Trenches Q.	1.7.16	7.20 A.M.	The battery of four Stoke's guns in emplacements at the end of the "Mary Tunnel" started firing on the German front line & communication trenches. They ceased fire at 7.32 A.M. The infantry started to advance at 7.30 A.M. The battery attached to the infantry (2 guns with the K.O.S.B. and 2 guns with the Border Reg.) went over with them but were held up before getting across "No man's land" at 8.45 P.M. We left the "Mary Tunnel" and took up an old defensive position in Cromwell Street and Piccadilly & Bond Street where we remained the night.	
"	2.7.16		The 87° Bgd. were taken out of the sector & went to the Hamel Trenches, the 87° T.M.B. being attached to the 88° Bgd. which relieved them. The artillery bombardment continued during the day but nothing of importance occurred.	
"	3.7.16		We remained in the defensive positions in Cromwell St. etc. & received orders to take battery to Englebelmer & myself to report to 87° Bgd. H.Q. at Hamel tomorrow morning.	
"	4.7.16		I took the battery to Englebelmer, reported at 87° Bgd. H.Q. at Hamel & went round the trenches in our new sector which are being held by K.O.S.B., Border Reg. & S.W.B., the Inniskilling being in reserve in Hamel. Then returned to Englebelmer.	
"	5.7.16		Brought the battery up from Englebelmer to Hamel. Found the trenches very wet after yesterdays rain. Started digging defensive emplacements.	

Army Form C. 2118.

87th T.M.B. (Cont.)

WAR DIARY
or
INTELLIGENCE SUMMARY.

(Erase heading not required.)

Instructions regarding War Diaries and Intelligence Summaries are contained in F. S. Regs., Part II. and the Staff Manual respectively. Title pages will be prepared in manuscript.

Place	Date	Hour	Summary of Events and Information	Remarks and references to Appendices
Trenches.	6.7.16		Digging emplacements and collecting and cleaning ammunition in the trenches. Took all the battery except 2 officers & gun crews back to artillery dugouts near Mesnil from where they will go up to the trenches every morning to work.	
	7.7.16		Digging emplacement. Very wet.	
	8.7.16		We were relieved today by the 88th T.M.B. and marched to Acheux Wood.	
Acheux.	9.7.16 to 16.7.16		In Acheux Wood tents.	
Trenches.	17.7.16		We marched to Englebelmer, and two batteries remained there while one went to relieve the 88th T.M.B. in the trenches. We continued working on emplacements started by them and cleaning ammunition.	
"	18.7.16 to 21.7.16		Working on emplacements and cleaning shells.	
	22.7.16 to 23.7.16		Commenced to dig a new emplacement for offensive purposes off the new firing line, also one in Fort Anley & one in Fort Wittington.	
Bus.	24.7.16		We were relieved in the trenches by the 74th Bgd. & marched to Bus where we stayed the night.	

1577 Wt. W10791/1773 500,000 1/15 D. D. & L. A.D.S.S./Forms/C. 2118.

Army Form C. 2118.

87th T.M.B. (Cav.)

WAR DIARY
or
INTELLIGENCE SUMMARY.
(Erase heading not required.)

Instructions regarding War Diaries and Intelligence Summaries are contained in F. S. Regs., Part II. and the Staff Manual respectively. Title pages will be prepared in manuscript.

Place	Date	Hour	Summary of Events and Information	Remarks and references to Appendices
Amplier	25.7.16		Marched from Rue to Amplier where we remain two nights.	
"	26.7.16		At Amplier huts.	
	27.7.16		Marched from Amplier to Doullens where we entrained for Rosan, arriving in the evening and marching to N. Camp.	
	28.7.16 to 31.7.16		In N. Camp, Rosan.	
	31.7.16		Relieved the 71st T.M.B. in Ypres salient.	

29th Division.
87th Infantry Brigade.

87th LIGHT TRENCH MORTAR BATTERY

AUGUST 1 9 1 6

CONFIDENTIAL.

WAR DIARY

OF

87th T.M. BATTERY.

From AUG. 1st To. AUG. 31st 1916.

(VOLUME 2)

87. T.M.B.

WAR DIARY
or
INTELLIGENCE SUMMARY
(Erase heading not required.)

Army Form C. 2118.

Hour, Date, Place	Summary of Events and Information	Remarks and references to Appendices
Wieltype S.c. Trenches Aug 1st	We have three guns mounted in New John St. one in S.10.A. one in X.8, three in S.8. & one in X.9. Everything quiet.	
Aug. 2nd	Working on new dug outs.	
" 3rd	Working on dug outs & improving emplacements. Nothing to report.	
" 7 "	Nothing to report.	
" 8 "	We were relieved by the 86th T.M.B. Before the relief took place, at about 11:15 P.M. we got the alarm (a gas attack, almost immediately our artillery started bombarding & put up a barrage in front) & in the German front line. We fired 11 shots from one of the guns in S.8. but ceased fire when we found the enemy was not getting out d his trenches. The Bombardment went on for about 2 hours. The 86th T.M.B. went up to the trenches to relieve us at 1:15, we then marched to 'C' camp Brandhoek.	
" 8 – 18 "	In 'C' Camp, Brandenhoek.	

87ᵗʰ T.M.B.

Army Form C. 2118

WAR DIARY
or
INTELLIGENCE SUMMARY
(Erase heading not required.)

Instructions regarding War Diaries and Intelligence Summaries are contained in F. S. Regs., Part II. and the Staff Manual respectively. Title pages will be prepared in manuscript.

Hour, Date, Place	Summary of Events and Information	Remarks and references to Appendices
Aug. 18ᵗʰ (Wulverghem)	Relieved 86ᵗʰ T.M.B. in the trenches.	
" 19ᵗʰ "	Quiet.	
" 20ᵗʰ "	Quiet. Lt. J. Anderson was killed by a H.V. shell in Garden St. 2nd Lt. Hannah took his place in the trenches.	
" 21ˢᵗ "	Nothing to report.	
" 22ⁿᵈ "	Quiet. 2nd Lt. Jacoby relieved 2nd Lt. Hannah.	
" 23ʳᵈ "	Prepared positions in A.8. to shoot at 'Kaiser Bill' from.	
" 24ᵗʰ–26ᵗʰ "	Nothing to report.	
" 27ᵗʰ "	Fired 5 rounds at listening post from New John Street.	
" 28ᵗʰ "	Nothing to report.	
" 29ᵗʰ "	Quiet.	
" 30ᵗʰ "	Fired 30 rounds at L.R.B. Cottage from New John St., and got several direct hits.	
" 31ˢᵗ "	Nothing to report.	

W.C. Gaskell Capt.
O.C. 87ᵗʰ T.M.B.